THE DUKERIES

&Sherwood Forest

This picture of 1788 by Francis Wheatley,
shows Henry Pelham–Clinton, 2nd Duke
of Newcastle returning from shooting in
the park at Clumber. His house seen in
the distance, was begun in 1768 and
demolished in 1938. The classical bridge
(see front cover), was built in 1770 and
still stands today.

By courtesy of the Private Collection/Bridgeman Art Library

The Gates of
Welbeck Abbey

contents

The Major Oak,
Edwinstowe

Pictures courtesy of Nottinghamshire County Council

THE DUKERIES

is a name used since the 18th century to describe a large area of Nottinghamshire which formerly contained the estates of four dukes. Because so much of this part of the Midlands was in the private ownership of enlightened noblemen, much of what is left of the once extensive Sherwood Forest has been preserved for the enjoyment of everyone.

Duke of Newcastle
(Clumber Park)

The National Trust property of Clumber Park is open at all times. Thoresby Hall has now been sympathetically renovated into a large historic hotel owned and managed by the Warner Holidays.

Duke of Kingston
(Thoresby Hall)

Rufford Abbey, once the family seat of Lord Savile, is largely demolished, but preservation work on what is left continues. Situated in what was formerly the stable block of the house, there is the Rufford Craft Centre. All of the Rufford property is now managed by Nottinghamshire County Council.

Lord Savile
(Rufford Abbey)

Welbeck Abbey remains completely unspoilt and was home of the Dukes of Portland. The Abbey itself is one of the largest and most splendid houses in the country. The Abbey is once again a family home (see p.36). There is no public access.

Duke of Portland
(Welbeck Abbey)

Although Worksop Manor is today a modest-sized country house, with no remarkable features, it was not always so. There was a time when Worksop was one of the largest mansions in the north and the property of the Dukes of Norfolk. Today the estate is in private hands with no public access.

Duke of Norfolk
(Worksop Manor)

Edwinstowe is the 'centre' for followers of Robin Hood and the Sherwood Forest Country Park and Visitor Centre incorporates 450 acres of ancient oaks including the celebrated 'Major Oak', Robin Hood's legendary hideout. Within an excellent programme of family events throughout the year there is the magnificent Robin Hood festival which takes place each summer.

Bess of Hardwick and some of her Ducal Descendants

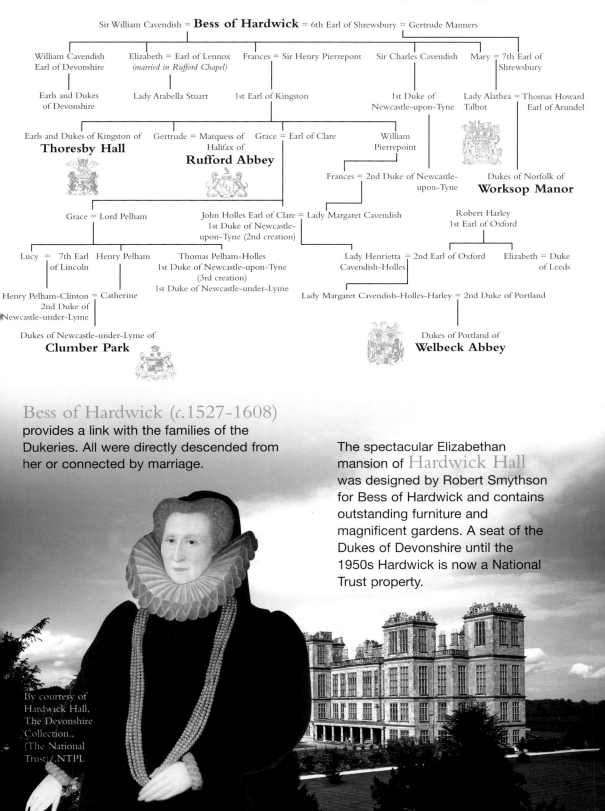

Sir William Cavendish = **Bess of Hardwick** = 6th Earl of Shrewsbury = Gertrude Manners

William Cavendish Earl of Devonshire

Elizabeth = Earl of Lennox *(married in Rufford Chapel)*

Frances = Sir Henry Pierrepont

Sir Charles Cavendish

Mary = 7th Earl of Shrewsbury

Earls and Dukes of Devonshire

Lady Arabella Stuart

1st Earl of Kingston

1st Duke of Newcastle-upon-Tyne

Lady Alathea Talbot = Thomas Howard Earl of Arundel

Earls and Dukes of Kingston of **Thoresby Hall**

Gertrude = Marquess of Halifax of **Rufford Abbey**

Grace = Earl of Clare

William Pierrepoint

Dukes of Norfolk of **Worksop Manor**

Frances = 2nd Duke of Newcastle-upon-Tyne

Grace = Lord Pelham

John Holles Earl of Clare = Lady Margaret Cavendish
1st Duke of Newcastle-upon-Tyne (2nd creation)

Robert Harley
1st Earl of Oxford

Lucy = 7th Earl of Lincoln

Henry Pelham

Thomas Pelham-Holles
1st Duke of Newcastle-upon-Tyne (3rd creation)
1st Duke of Newcastle-under-Lyme

Lady Henrietta = 2nd Earl of Oxford
Cavendish-Holles

Elizabeth = Duke of Leeds

Henry Pelham-Clinton = Catherine
2nd Duke of Newcastle-under-Lyme

Lady Margaret Cavendish-Holles-Harley = 2nd Duke of Portland

Dukes of Newcastle-under-Lyme of **Clumber Park**

Dukes of Portland of **Welbeck Abbey**

Bess of Hardwick (*c.*1527–1608)

provides a link with the families of the Dukeries. All were directly descended from her or connected by marriage.

The spectacular Elizabethan mansion of Hardwick Hall was designed by Robert Smythson for Bess of Hardwick and contains outstanding furniture and magnificent gardens. A seat of the Dukes of Devonshire until the 1950s Hardwick is now a National Trust property.

By courtesy of Hardwick Hall, The Devonshire Collection, (The National Trust)/.NTPL

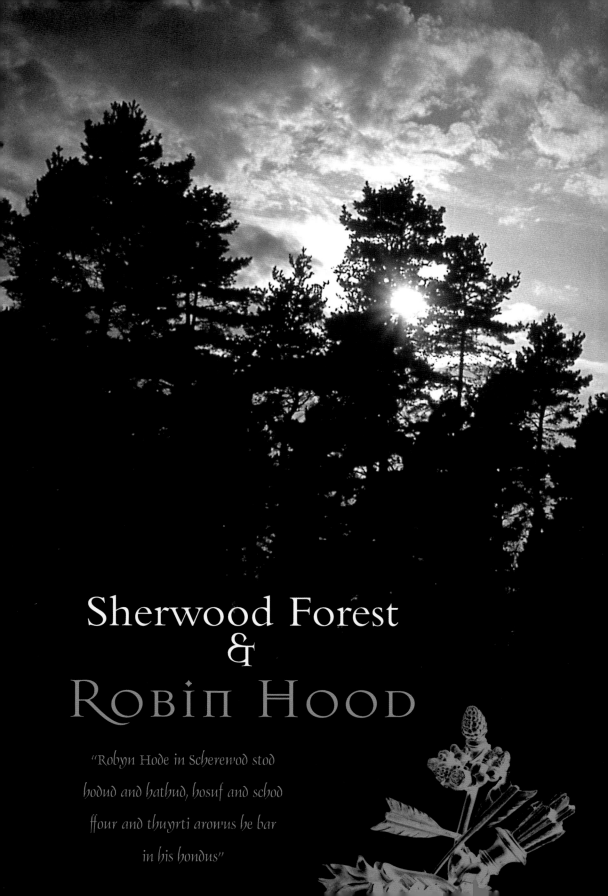

Sherwood Forest
&
ROBIN HOOD

"Robyn Hode in Scherewod stod

hodud and hathud, hosuf and schod

ffour and thuyrti arowus he bar

in his hondus"

Sherwood Forest, in the minds of most people, is inseparably linked with the legends of Robin Hood and his companions. Whether he really was the swashbuckling Errol Flynn-style hero robbing the rich and helping the poor, whether he was simply what would now be called a 'thief' or indeed whether he actually existed at all is unlikely ever to be resolved.

But there is no better place to start your search for Robin Hood than the Sherwood Forest Visitor Centre at Edwinstowe.

The Major Oak

~ legend has it that the famous outlaw used this tree as his hideout. Today this ancient tree is a great tourist attraction for visitors from around the world.

At the Sherwood Forest Visitor Centre the history of the forest and its connection with the Robin Hood legend are told in the "Robyn Hode's Sherwode" exhibition. There are miles of beautiful walks through vast tracts of unspoilt countryside, the Mighty Major Oak and the Forest Table Restaurant for relaxation and refreshments afterwards.

Robin Hood's name may have been a general term for an outlaw - a 'Robin o'th' Woods'- living on his wits at a time when outlawing was part of the medieval criminal code. It would be pleasant to be able to believe in him as a real person, and with evidence of a 'Robyn Hode' found as far back as the 14th century, it may well be that there is a basis of truth in the whole thing. After all the existence of King Arthur, considered to be legendary, has now almost irrefutably been proved by archaeology. Robin actually has an entry in the Dictionary of National Biography which says that his historical authenticity is 'ill-supported'. He first appears in Wyntoun's 'Chronicle of Scotland' in about 1420, and this was probably based on oral traditions. Robin figures largely in literature, but the fact that the main work about him 'The Lyttle Geste of Robyn Hode' appeared from Caxton's press at Westminster in 1495 some three hundred years after the alleged goings on in Sherwood Forest make establishing his existence much more difficult. He is located in the 'Lyttle Geste', in Yorkshire and only later ballads and stories move him to Nottinghamshire. King Arthur, of course, is claimed by numerous areas of Britain from Cornwall to Midlothian.

In the seventeenth and eighteenth centuries Robin Hood lore became more popular and several plays were written around him. 'The True Tale of Robin Hood' in verse appeared in 1632 which has him dying on 18th November 1247 while Joseph Hunter the eminent author of 'Hallamshire' and 'South Yorkshire' considered that he was a contemporary of Edward II.

To some he is a popular hero of the common people - the thorn in the side of what would now be called 'The Establishment'- sheriffs, barons and prelates, yet other legends make him a renegade noble - an Earl of Huntingdon no less. A huge grave in the churchyard at Hathersage in Derbyshire is reputed to be of 'Little John', but the headstone and railings are Victorian.

A splendid poem 'Robin Hood and Guy of Gisburne' will be found in Percy's 'Reliques of Ancient English Poetry' and all the confused literature and theories about the character may well be founded on oral traditions with a firm basis of truth and it would be churlish indeed to dismiss Robin as being altogether a myth.

Edwinstowe is the forest village where Robin Hood and Maid Marian were supposed to have been married. North of the village lies the greatest tract remaining of Sherwood Forest with many fine specimens of ancient oaks. Most notable of these is the Major Oak. It was named after the local antiquarian, Major Rooke, who was very fond of the tree and the locals referred to it as 'Major's Oak' which soon became simply the Major Oak. Before 1800 it was more generally known as the Queen Oak and it is now the largest oak surviving in Sherwood but in spite of its girth of 32' 10" is still only the 20th largest in England.

Like other heavily forested areas, Sherwood was popular with the Kings of England who were able to find much good sport here. King John, who actually preferred Rockingham Forest, had a hunting lodge near Clipstone, the ruins of which are known as 'King John's Palace'. The King held an emergency Parliament here in 1200. Subsequent monarchs visited the Forest including Edward I who also summoned a Parliament at Clipstone, Edward II who held Court there, and Edward III.

Several spectacular bird of prey species breed here and visit on passage. One of the most notable being the

Honey Buzzard

which has been a regular summer visitor for many years to sites in the Dukeries. A relative of our resident Common Buzzard it takes its name from its habit of feeding on large insects especially bees, hence 'honey'.

Paul Doherty / RSPB-images.com

Wildlife
of the area

The Dukeries as an area is characterised by several kinds of habitat: large areas of conifer plantations, ancient mixed woodland, bracken and gorse heathland with silver birch and several lakes and waterways. All these support a surprisingly rich variety of wildlife, especially birds. The illusive and mysterious

Nightjar is a summer visitor from Africa and nests at a few heathland locations such as the heathland at Sherwood Pines Forest Park, where the shy Fallow Deer can also be seen. Both Green and Great spotted woodpeckers are regularly sighted with most of this country's woodland species, and the several lakes are home to a variety of waterbirds and wildfowl such as these Canada Geese being fed beside the lake at Clumber.

Drake and duck Mallard

Green woodpecker

Great spotted woodpecker

Mute Swan

Worksop

Worksop is a good place to start a tour of the Dukeries. Travelling south on the B6034 the entrances to both Clumber and Thoresby will be found on the left.

The jewel of Worksop is the Priory Church of Our Lady and St. Cuthbert, a magnificent Norman building with a unique gatehouse. Although a parish church existed earlier, the monastery was founded in 1103 by the Lord of the Manor, Sir William de Lovetot, and the nave completed in 1170. Three mutilated effigies of Lord Furnival and his sister and brother-in-law Sir Thomas and Lady Nevill can be seen near the south transept.

During the 1539 dissolutions Worksop was lucky, for although all the monastic buildings were destroyed the main priory church remained, though reduced in size, together with the wonderful Gatehouse and its shrine. Even after passing to the Augustinians, the Priory remained the parish church as it had been since 1103 which is why it survived and is used for the same purpose today. Restoration work was carried out on the Priory in the 1920s and 1930s and thanks to a handsome legacy from a former Worksop choirboy, John F. Ellis, new additions in modern style have been made to the east end during the 1970s.

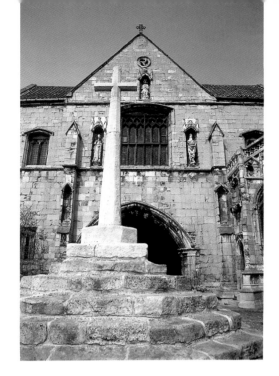

The Gatehouse

is one of the most interesting buildings in the county and is late 13th century. The exterior is decorated by niches containing statues which somehow escaped the iconoclasts. They depict St. Augustine, St. Cuthbert and other religious imagery. The

south east corner has a decorated projection which was a shrine probably containing a holy relic and a statue of Our Lady. The Gatehouse is now an Art Gallery and Exhibition Centre, incorporating a tea room.

Creswell Crags

Creswell Crags is a miniature Cheddar Gorge with impressive limestone cliffs much covered with greenery and containing numerous caves. This quiet beauty spot soon became renowned as a place to discover startling evidence of a prehistoric past after Victorian archaeologists uncovered the bone remains of animals roaming in England during the Ice Age, animals like hyaena, woolly mammoth, rhinoceros, reindeer and other wiled beasts. Our ancient ancestors

also sheltered in the caves indicated by stone and bone tools and some of the earliest bone engraving which they left behind in the caves.

The Museum and Education Centre at one end of the site contains an exhibition and audio visual displays, which describes the Ice Age history of the site, a gift shop and has full facilities

Creswell Crags is south west of Worksop and can be reached from the B6042 off the A60, north west of the village of Holbeck.

One of the caves bears the name *Robin Hood.* It was to here that Edward II was said to have pursued Robin Hood after first imprisoning several peasant families in the dungeons of his palace at nearby Clipstone.

The Harley Gallery, Welbeck

Other Attractions

Within the area, there are a great many attractive and interesting places to visit.

The award winning Harley Gallery at Welbeck is a showcase for contemporary arts and crafts. There is a Craft Shop selling work from across the country and a Coffee Bar, all set in a relaxing environment.

The market town of Mansfield is a good shopping centre. One of the more interesting places to visit is the White Lion Yard and its caves which has recently benefited from restoration funding, and is now an exciting and educational experience. Aficianados is a café restaurant set into a cave.

The White Lion Yard, Mansfield

In this quiet unspoilt area of Nottinghamshire there are many traditional English villages which have a charm all of their own. Carburton has one of the smallest parish churches in the country, at Clipstone there are the remains of King John's hunting lodge, known as King John's Palace. Holbeck is a small hamlet on the Welbeck estate and in the private church of St Winifred several members of the Portland family are buried. Near to Markham Clinton is the mausoleum of the 4th Duke of Newcastle and his Duchess, designed by Robert Smirke, architect of the British Museum.

Wellow is an unspoilt village with a wide village green and one of the few surviving permanent maypoles in England. There is still dancing round the maypole once a year, usually on Whit Monday, but that date is sometimes changed.

Edwinstowe has a fine church dating from the 12th and 13th centuries in which, it is said, the marriage took place between Robin Hood and Maid Marian.

Unspoilt English villages

By courtesy of Notts C.C.

Traditional festivals

By courtesy of Notts C.C.

The Robin Hood Festival

By courtesy of Notts C.C.

Stunning scenery and wildlife

Clumber Park has 3,800 acres to enjoy. It is a favourite
venue throughout the year for walkers, cyclists, bird watchers
and lovers of peace and quiet.

Clumber
and its history

Clumber Park is National Trust property and open at all times. It is one of the largest country parks in Europe and covers over 3,800 acres. The lake extends to 87 acres, 1,000 acres are woodland and the park's perimeter is over 10 miles in length. There are miles of walks and drives, a shop and a restaurant and plenty of places for parking and picnicking.

Through the grand classical screen of Apleyhead Lodge on the A614 about six miles north of Ollerton, the approach to Clumber is highly impressive, for what Clumber lacks in interesting buildings it makes up for with the famous three-mile long Duke's Drive, or Lime Tree Avenue. One of the finest in Europe, it consists of double rows of magnificent limes leading towards what was once an immense house built in 1770 - the former seat of the Dukes of Newcastle-under-Lyme. Today only a tiny fragment is left standing together with the stables and clocktower.

Fortunately the family's large private church, built by the 7th Duke of Newcastle in 1884, still stands close to the site of the house.

The dukedom of Newcastle was connected with Welbeck in the person of William Cavendish, 1st Duke of Newcastle-upon-Tyne. The dukedom became extinct and was revived for the son-in-law of the 2nd Duke, John Holles, Earl of Clare who became 1st

Building of the Chapel of St. Mary the Virgin, was begun by the 7th Duke in 1886 to the designs of G. F. Bodley and completed in 1889. As large as a parish church, it is constructed from local white Steetley stone with contrasting details in red sandstone from Runcorn in Cheshire. The magnificent spire rises to 180 feet.

The chapel is in the parish of Worksop and is used by local people and visitors alike.

Thomas Pelham-Holles,
1st Duke of Newcastle of the third creation (1693-1768), sharing what looks like an 18th century bottle of chianti, with, on the right, his brother-in-law, Henry Clinton, 7th Earl of Lincoln (1684-1728). The later Dukes of Newcastle were descended from the 7th Earl's son Henry Pelham-Clinton, the 2nd Duke of Newcastle-under-Lyme.

By courtesy of the National Portrait Gallery

One of Clumber's magnificent
'wilderness' areas

Rufford Abbey
and its history

The remains of this 12th century abbey and
later country house, are the centre of a 150
acre country park with attractions such as a
Craft Shop, Gallery, Ceramic Centre and a
permanent exhibition on the monastic
history of the site. There are also gardens,
extensive woodlands, an arboretum and lake,
and there are on-site shops and the Coach
House Cafe and the Victorian-style
Savile Restaurant.

Rufford has entrances near the old
main gates to the house on the
A614 south of Ollerton, and on the
Wellow Road.

The once great house of Rufford displayed examples of every kind of English architectural style from the 12th to the 19th centuries, both ecclesiastical and secular.

The story of the decline and fall of Rufford Abbey is a long and distressing one. Had conservation funding been as available as it is today, the building could have been spared its partial demolition in the mid 1950s. However, the local authority is now continuing to sympathetically renovate and restore what remains.

The earliest architectural work is the 12th century undercroft of the original abbey. It was mainly through the existence of this crypt that the surviving fabric of the later buildings above ground have been preserved to protect the medieval stonework beneath.

In 1148 Gilbert de Gant, Earl of Lincoln, founded here an offshoot of Rievaulx Abbey in Yorkshire for a group of Cistercians. The monks remained in occupation until 1536 when the Abbey and its lands passed to secular ownership. In 1537 the fee simple was acquired by the 6th Earl of Shrewsbury, Bess of Hardwick's fourth husband.

The story of Bess of Hardwick's ambitious schemes for her children is well known, but her most daring coup was the engineered marriage between her daughter Elizabeth to the young Earl of Lennox, brother of Lord Darnley and close in line of succession to the throne. The marriage took place in the private chapel at Rufford, a room which in the 1950s was still hung with tapestries and containing heraldic glass commemorating this unfortunate event. Two years after the ceremony at Rufford the Earl died aged 21 leaving an only child, the tragic Lady Arabella Stuart. She was considered as a risk to both Elizabeth and James and died in the Tower, an innocent pawn in the power game of monarchy and politics.

The ghost of Lady Arabella is supposed to have stalked the corridors of Rufford, along with a number of other apparitions. It was said that Rufford was one of the most haunted houses in England, one manifestation being a cold, clammy baby which had the disconcerting habit of getting into bed with you.

Rufford was one of Shrewsbury's estates which Bess did not get her hands on as after his death it passed to his daughter Lady Mary Talbot who was married to Sir George Savile, a Yorkshire baronet. Had the great-grandson of this marriage been more self-seeking and line-toeing it is certain that Rufford could have been truly one of the Dukeries. Geographically it is so but no owner ever actually achieved a dukedom, though George Savile would have done had he not attempted to steady the country at the time of the 1688 troubles. As it was he became the Marquess of Halifax and one of the most distinguished figures in the troubled times at the end of the seventeenth century. None deserved a dukedom more than he, so it is fitting that Rufford should at any rate be considered as an honorary member of the Dukeries.

Lord Halifax was responsible for the above mentioned Stuart north wing of the Abbey. He was a man who was dictated to by his conscience and he never hesitated to oppose measures whether Whig or Tory which he thought damaging to his country. Not for nothing was he known to history as 'The Trimmer'. His second wife was a Pierrepont from Thoresby and through her he was grandfather of the celebrated 4th Earl of Chesterfield.

The marquessate became extinct with the death of the second Lord Halifax and the Savile property passed to another George Savile, a cousin who succeeded as sixth baronet in 1700.

The eighth baronet was an M.P. and had a distinguished career of public service. Like his great kinsman 'The Trimmer' he was an unbiased and patriotic politician. He saw how things were going in the American colonies, and his advice, had it been accepted, would probably have prevented the War of Independence. He warned both sides and offered advice to both without showing favour to either. Sir George was the last of his line. On his premature death in 1784 his estates were divided between his niece Mrs. Foljambe, whose descendants took the name of Savile-Foljambe, and his nephew the Hon. John Lumley, son of his sister Barbara and the third Earl

The gates of Rufford on the A614, south of Ollerton, surmounted by the arms of the 7th Earl of Scarbrough : Savile quartering Lumley. At the top of the coronet is a swan feeding its young and the arms are supported by two parrots.

TOP:
Rufford Abbey from the north-west as it appeared when the Savile family still occupied the House.

MIDDLE:
The splendid Great Hall before the 1938 sale.

BOTTOM:
The old Rufford saw mill.

BELOW:
Rufford Craft Centre.

of Scarbrough. John Lumley eventually succeeded as seventh Earl of Scarbrough and took the name of Savile-Lumley. He came into all the Yorkshire and Nottinghamshire properties.

The Earl was a parson and prebendary of York. He never took his seat in the Lords and died in a hunting accident in 1856. His son and successor, the 8th Earl, died unmarried, but he left five illegitimate sons by a French woman. He bequeathed Rufford to the second of these sons, Henry Savile-Lumley, a keen sportsman and racehorse owner whose famous horse 'Cremorne' won the Derby and the Ascot Cup. This superb animal is buried in an animal cemetery to the north of the Abbey.

Eventually the eldest illegitimate son, John Savile-Lumley, inherited Rufford. He had a long, distinguished diplomatic career and while British Ambassador in Rome he carried out important excavations. A replica of an enormous fountain discovered during his work still exists adjacent to the Orangery. When John Savile retired he was raised to the Peerage as Baron Savile. He had dropped the name Lumley on succeeding to the Rufford estates.

As he was unmarried, the title was specially remaindered so as to pass to his nephew. Lord Savile was a patron of the Arts and an artist himself, and it was he who commissioned Salvin to alter the house. He collected many of the treasures which were later to be dispersed at the 1938 sale.

The 2nd Lord Savile reversed his name to Lumley-Savile. He was a friend of King Edward VII who several times visited the Abbey for the Doncaster races and for shooting. On one

Charles II

occasion Lord Savile employed Sir Harry Lauder to entertain his royal guest and when the King died he erected a sundial to his memory. James I and Charles II both stayed at Rufford.

Within living memory Rufford was an estate and great house in full swing with the usual complements of servants, stable hands, gardeners and foresters. It all ended in 1938 when the present Lord Savile parted with his Rufford estates. An enormous sale of building and contents took place and the estate itself passed from the family which had held it for almost exactly four hundred years.

Rutford was bought by industrialist, Sir Albert Ball, father of the famous V.C. of the same name. His executors sold out to Mr. Henry Talbot de Vere Clifton who wished to build a large housing development there but was prevented from doing so.

Now the ruins of the Abbey are the centrepiece to Rufford Country Park and Craft Centre, open to the public and managed by Nottinghamshire County Council. The lake, once emptied as a result of coal mining beneath it, has been re-filled and stocked with wildlife including wildfowl. Visitor amenities at the old sawmill include the Outdoor Living Store and Lakeside Garden Shop.

The ford at Rufford Mill.

Thoresby Hall

Thoresby Hall is a magnificent Grade 1 listed building, built for the 3rd Earl Manvers during the 1860s by the renowned architect of the day Anthony Salvin. Today it has been fully restored to its former glory by Warner Holidays Ltd., and is now one of their Historic Hotels.

Day visitors can look around the magnificent interiors and stroll round the grounds. Thoresby Gallery, part of Thoresby Estate is also open to day visitors. There are Cafes and a Restaurant and a Leisure Complex with a range of facilities including a swimming pool.

A detail from Tillemans painting of 1725 showing the original Thoresby Hall, designed by William Talman, the architect of Chatsworth. *Below:* Arms of the 6th and last Earl Manvers

Thoresby Hall was rebuilt by the 3rd Earl Manvers abandoning the largish comfortable old mansion by the lake and commissioning the brilliant and fashionable architect Anthony Salvin - who also worked on the house at Rufford - to design him a romantic Elizabethan palace on the scale of Burghley House near Stamford. Though he built a house planned to stand for a thousand years he could not have known that in less than a century social revolution would make such houses anachronisms and that the sturdy walls would crack as a result of coal mining far beneath. Sir Henry Pierrepont in *c.*1290 married the heiress Annora de Manvers of Holme near Nottingham. This property was to be their descendants' principal seat for several centuries and became known as Holme Pierrepont, and though the name of Manvers disappeared it was

resurrected in the 19th century as will be seen. Holme Pierrepont is still occupied by descendants of the Manvers family and is open to the public. The son of Henry and Annora, Robert, became Governor of Newark Castle, and the family connection with that town was also perpetuated later when, in 1627, the then head of the family, Robert Pierrepont, was created Lord Pierrepont, Viscount Newark and later Earl of Kingston. It was the lst Earl of Kingston who acquired the estate of Thoresby which hitherto had passed through the hands of many different families. William Talman, the architect of Chatsworth, was brought in to design the first Thoresby Hall.

Lord Kingston was an ardent Royalist in the Civil War though earlier he had sat on the fence and declared that he would rather be torn in two than take

sides in the conflict. In due course
loyalty won and he joined the Royalists
but he was later taken prisoner by Lord
Willoughby of Parham who put the Earl
in a small boat bound for Kingston-on-
Hull - the only town in Yorkshire which
was not for the King, an irony surpassed
only by the unfortunate man being
literally cut in half by a Royalist cannon
ball fired at the boat as it sailed up the
Humber.

The 2nd Earl of Kingston was also a
Royalist and adhered to Charles I,
accompanying him to Oxford. Two years
after succeeding to his father's titles, he
was himself created Marquess of
Dorchester. Scholarly and eccentric, he
was a man of violent temper and much
addicted to duels.

Evelyn 1st Duke of Kingston (left), Charles
2nd Earl of Burlington and Lord Berkeley of
Stratton by Michael Dahl.

Lady Mary Wortley-Montagu
née Pierrepont.

The marquessate became extinct, but
the earldom was inherited by three
great-nephews in turn, the third of whom
became the 5th Earl of Kingston. He was
Evelyn Pierrepont, a prominent man of
fashion and a firm Hanoverian. Queen
Anne regranted him the extinct
marquessate of Dorchester and on the
succession of George I he was made a
Privy Councillor and raised to the rank of
Duke of Kingston. He was handsome
and clever without being brilliant, but his
daughter, Lady Mary Pierrepont (see top
of page), made her mark in the annals of
both medicine and literature. She eloped
with Edward Wortley-Montagu, a
diplomat, and spent some time in Turkey
where she observed a primitive form of
inoculation among the natives. This she
courageously tried on her own infant,
thus saving him from smallpox. In spite
of being hounded and ridiculed by the

Church, the medical profession and her neighbours, Lady Mary, like Dr. Jenner, fought to introduce smallpox immunisation into England against incredible prejudice.

Evelyn Pierrepont (right),
2nd Duke of Kingston

Lady Mary's brother never lived to inherit and the dukedom went to the Ist Duke's grandson, Evelyn Pierrepont (illustrated above), 2nd Duke of Kingston. This Duke went through a ceremony of marriage with Elizabeth Chudleigh who had been secretly married to the Hon. Augustus Hervey, an impoverished naval lieutenant. The marriage was a disaster and when Hervey found that he would soon become Earl of Bristol, he decided to get rid of his wife, a somewhat scandalously behaved woman, and sued for divorce. Elizabeth denied that the marriage had taken place and a court ruled that she was technically a spinster. She had, for some time, been the mistress of the Duke of Kingston who

then 'married' her, died and left her all his property for life. The dukedom became extinct, but there was an ultimate heir to the Duke's fortune - his nephew Charles Meadows who instituted proceedings for bigamy against the 'Duchess'. As she was by now legally Countess of Bristol, she was tried by the House of Lords and found guilty. Meadows succeeded to the Kingston estates immediately and adopted the name and arms of Pierrepont. In 1796, he was created Baron Pierrepont and Viscount Newark. It would have been pleasant to have had the earldom of Kingston re-created for him, but some years before, the King family had been made Earls of Kingston in the peerage of Ireland. Meadows, now Pierrepont, went back for his title to the marriage centuries before which brought the Pierreponts their first permanent family home - the marriage with Annora de Manvers. The new Viscount Newark was, in 1807, created Earl Manvers. The title became extinct in 1955 on the death of the 6th and last Earl Manvers. Mr. Hugh Matheson, one of the heirs to the Thoresby estate, has built a Palladian villa not far from the old house.

A fascinating and lavishly illustrated new guidebook to Thoresby Hall Historic Hotel is available at the Hotel

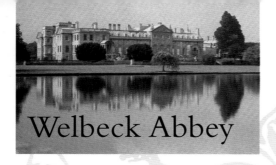

Welbeck Abbey

The Abbey is now the home of William Parente, Prince of Castel Viscardo and his family. He is the grandson of the 7th Duke of Portland, and both the House and the grounds are strictly private. However, walkers and cyclists may take the Robin Hood way for 4 miles through the estate. Towards the end of the walk the path runs beside the raised line of one of the underground gas-lit tunnels, built by the Duke through the park and under the lake.

Welbeck Abbey was once one of the richest in England. Following its

dissolution, it eventually came into the hands of William Cavendish, grandson of Bess of Hardwick. Created 1st Duke of Newcastle upon Tyne, he was a passionate royalist and became known as the Loyal Duke. He entertained Charles I lavishly at Welbeck. His sons having died without male issue, Welbeck passed to Margaret Cavendish

Harley, who in 1734 married William Bentinck, 2nd Duke of Portland. Their son, the 3rd Duke, was twice Prime Minister. His heir the 4th Duke, achieved national renown by creating England's first sewage farm at the Flood Meadows in Clipstone. Lord William John Cavendish Scott Bentinck succeeded him in 1854. Stories of the 5th Duke of Portland abound. A shy recluse, thwarted in love by an opera singer, he spent colossal sums at Welbeck on extraordinary building work above and below ground, while the Duke himself virtually camped out in a handful of rooms. Such was the unending chaos, that the 6th Duke, who inherited in 1879, considered abandoning Welbeck. However, by 1881 sufficient progress had been made for him to invite the Prince of Wales to a great party, the first of many over some 63 years - Welbeck's golden age. A racing man the Duke had winners in the Derby, Oaks and St Leger, but he and his wife also had a reputation for charitable works. The Orthopaedic Hospital at Harlow Wood, for example, came into being through their efforts. In 1943 Welbeck passed to the 7th Duke whose surviving daughter, Lady Anne Bentinck, still lives on the estate. With the death of the 9th Duke in 1990 the dukedom became extinct.

Information courtesy of Bassetlaw District Council

The 6th Duke of Portland constructed this monument to Lord George Bentinck, the celebrated 19th century Tory politician and racing man. A potential Prime Minister, he was only 47 when he suddenly died near this spot while walking from Welbeck to Thoresby. The monument can be seen by the road that runs next to the river Poulter between Norton and Carburton.

TOP and ABOVE: The Riding School at Welbeck was built by the 5th Duke of Portland (right), and in its day was second only in size to the celebrated Spanish Riding School in Vienna.

The Gates of Welbeck Abbey

Worksop Manor

The present manor is a relatively small private residence and neither house nor grounds are open to the public.

Following its dissolution the Priory was closed in 1539 and all monastic land became the property of the Earl of Shrewsbury, Lord of the Manor of Worksop.

The 4th Earl's "fair lodge at Wyrksoppe Park" was swallowed up by the 6th Earl's magnificent, towering late 16th century mansion, designed by Robert Smythson, architect of nearby Hardwick Hall - the 6th Earl was Bess of Hardwick's last husband.

Worksop Manor, which was one of the largest in England with over 500 rooms, as it appeared before the devastating fire of 1761 which completely destroyed it.

It was by marriage that Worksop Manor passed to the Dukes of Norfolk. The 8th Duke, who succeeded in 1701, modernised the house, but in 1761 it was burnt down. A new palace was designed in Palladian style, the largest country house commissioned since Blenheim. However, with only one wing completed, the death of the 9th Duke's nephew and heir from measles in 1767 put a stop to building. Even so, the single wing was impressive and the park, eight miles round, contained a lake, temple, menagerie and fine woodlands.

Following the Duke's own death ten years later at the age of 91, succeeding Dukes rarely came to Worksop. The 12th Duke carried out repairs but sold the estate to the Duke of Newcastle for £375,000. Apart from the service block it was then demolished.

While Lord and Lady Foley (daughter of the 13th Duke of Norfolk) lived on the estate in the remodelled servants' quarters, lovely gardens were created. It was not until 1890, when the Worksop Manor estate was sold by the 7th Duke of Newcastle, that it ceased being a ducal seat. Under its new owner, Sir John Robinson, once High Sheriff of Nottinghamshire and a keen horseman, the estate became a noted stud. Sir John's descendants still live on the property.

Information courtesy of Bassetlaw District Council

A double portrait of Mary Queen of Scots and her son James I of England and James VI of Scotland. Mary was kept captive at Worksop in 1583 and following the death of Elizabeth I in 1603, her son the new King James I stayed at the manor on his way from Scotland to London.

Lords of the Manor at Worksop provided the right hand glove for the sovereign at Coronations and to support the Royal arm so long as it held the sceptre. The 9th Duke of Newcastle, however, was refused the claim to provide the glove at the last coronation as the manorial rights were vested in a limited company.

The completed North wing of Worksop Manor before the demolition over a century ago.

Walks

in the Dukeries

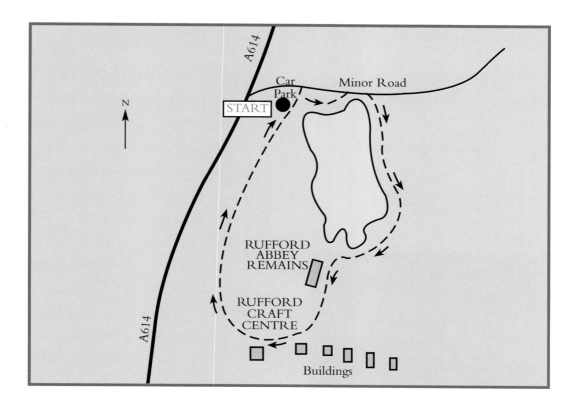

Walk 1: Rufford Lake

Walk Time: 50mins

Distance: 3km 1.9miles

Start: Car park at north end
of lake GR 646657

A pleasant walk with numerous points
of interest on route.

1. From the car park walk through the
   opening to the lake then turn left
   passing the buildings and old mill.

2. Follow path, walking clockwise
   around the lake, passing over
   wooden walkways on route.

You emerge on a path at the
opposite side leading to the abbey
ruins. Continue on this to the far
end where you see the sign for
'The Orangery'.

3. Turn right walking between the
   buildings to the car park at the
   south end. Walk through the
   car park to meet a path leading
   off right. This area is called
   'The Wilderness'.

4. This straight path goes through
   woodland back to the north
   end car park.

Walk 2: Sherwood Forest & Budby

Walk Time: 1hr 45mins

Distance: 8.1km 5.0miles

Start:

Visitor Centre car park GR 627676

A good, generally flat walk on forest tracks.

1 From Car Park walk towards the visitor centre in Sherwood Forest, bear left at the entrance. A sign states 'Waymarked Paths start here'. Take the left path, which is the Birklands Ramble.

2. Walk along the wide path passing old oak trees. You soon see an open field through the trees on your left. You come to a major junction on the path. A sign points right to the Major Oak but continue straight ahead for 50m to a metal barrier where you bear right (not to Major Oak).

3. The path descends slightly for a short distance, 500m further on you come to a point where 4 paths meet. Take the second-left path, which is a bridleway, marked by a horseshoe sign. Continue to a fork in the path bearing left still on the bridleway.

4. Pass public bridleway sign; you come to a crossroads with a metal barrier across the path ahead. Turn right here leading to an open area. You may see a seat nearby as you descend on the wide track for 200m. Continue on the main track ahead keeping the forest on your left for 900m. You arrive at a wide crossroads at the corner of the forest/open area. A green public bridleway sign points right to Budby. Follow this on the wide track passing a conservation area on your left.

5. You come to the corner of Ladysmith Plantation. Continue straight ahead passing two metal 5-bar gates together on your right. To your left you see the rooftops of the houses in Budby.

6. The track is slightly undulating as you come to a grass track, on a slight bend, leading to the left. Bear

left onto the grass track walking towards the main road. Turn right on a narrow faint path 25m from the road and walk parallel with the road for 800m in a southeast direction to the next road junction.

7. Turn right back towards the Major Oak walking along the roadside for 500m in a southerly direction to just past the corner of Sherwood Forest on your right.

8. You see two 5-bar gates on the right with an opening at the side of them. Go through following this path to the Major Oak. The path forks after 250m, take the left fork.

9. On reaching the main circular path at the Major Oak follow this and the signposts back to the Visitor Centre.

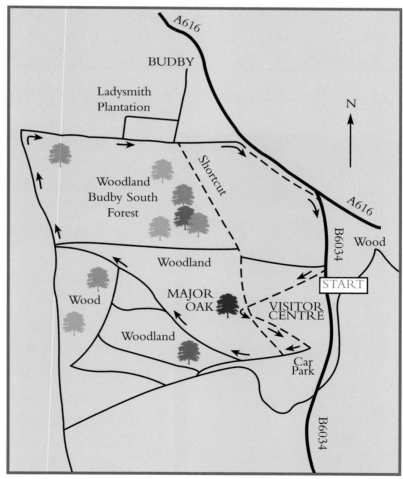

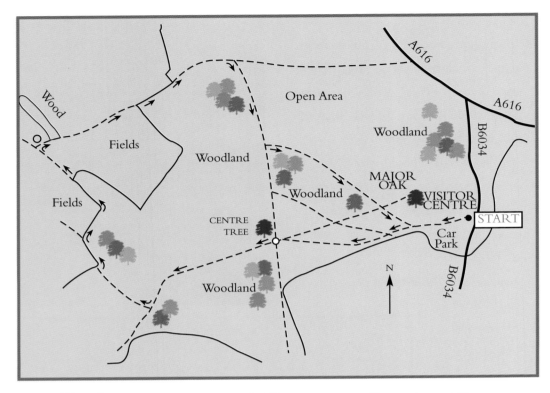

Walk 3: Sherwood Forest - Centre Tree

Walk Time: 2hrs 45min

Distance: 13.9km 8.64miles

Start: Visitor Centre car park GR 627676

A good flat walk on forest tracks.

1. From the Visitor Centre, keep left looking for a sign 'Waymarked Paths start here'. Take the left path, which is the Birklands Ramble.

2. Walk on the wide path, passing some old oak trees, to a metal barrier. Go through the barrier, there are open fields to the left and woodland to the right.

3. 350m past the barrier pass a path bearing right; continue for another 250m to the next path branching off right. Follow this for 900m to meet another track, turn left for 50m to a distinctive tree in a clearing. This tree is known as Centre Tree.

4. Continue now in same direction (E.S.E) for 1.2km to a wide track junction. Turn left for 350m then right descending Top Vals Hill on a wide track a further 250m. On a bend at the bottom, look for a Public Footpath sign across Bottom Vals Hill in a N.W direction, for 500m to a corner of woodland/open fields.

5. Walk ahead keeping the wood on your right with open field to the left. At next corner of wood turn right along a track, still keeping the wood on your right for 460m to a corner of Ling Plantation.

6. Turn left still on a track for 1km, soon with open fields on both sides, to arrive at the corner of Broomhill Lane. Turn right here following the bridleway past the sewage works then between open fields for 1.1km to the corner of Gleadthorpe New Plantation.

7. Walk along keeping the forest on your right for 400m. Stay on the main bridleway which goes through the forest and bears right to the far side.

8. On reaching an open area at Budby South Forest turn right for 1km keeping forest to right with field to left. At far end walk 150m into forest turn left then bear right after 220m on a bridleway which passes the Major Oak on your way back to the car park 2.3km further on.

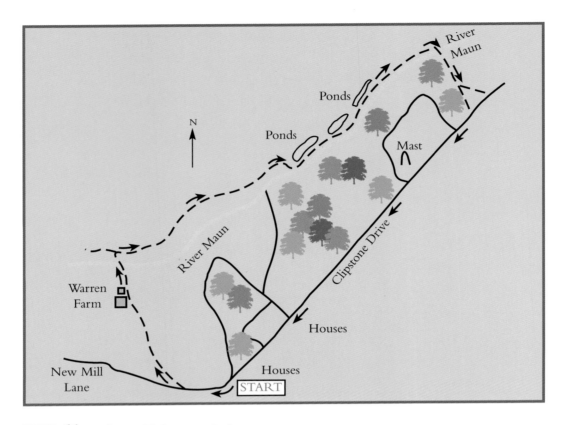

Walk 4: River Maun

Walk Time: 1hr 25mins

Distance: 7.2km 4.5miles

Start / Park:

New Mill Lane PF sign GR 568627

A good, mostly flat and interesting walk by the River Maun, incorporating field, river and woodland.

1. You see an obvious narrow path descending across the field. Continue to far side then before you reach a large tree another path bears off left ascending to an old 5-bar gate.

2. Walk into next field then along by right side of a hedge towards Warren Farm which you may see 500m ahead.

3. Approaching the farm, keep to the right side of it walking behind the barn on your right. You see a small stile and broken fence behind the barn where you turn right onto a track descending to the River Maun, 200m further on.

4. Cross the small bridge then ascend the track for 70m to just before another small bridge over a disused canal. Turn right onto a farm track, which runs parallel with the River Maun and winds its way along the valley. Continue on this track for 1.5km until you arrive at two 5-bar gates ahead.

5. Turn sharp right to descend for 200m to the River Maun at GR 577641 then left at the river to pass a number of small fishing lakes at Newlands.

6. You pass a bridge across the river on your right, do not cross that bridge but continue 1km further to a white 5-bar gate and railings next to a camp site.

7. Turn right over a small bridge crossing the River Maun at GR 587649. You ascend now

through Cavendish Wood on a track leading to Clipstone Drive. After 250m the path forks and you take the right fork to ascend to a wide track. The track winds right then levels out as you leave the wood. You may see some new houses across an open field.

8. You are now walking on a long straight track for 2.5km; this eventually turns to a road at the far end. Stay on this track passing behind a row of houses in the same direction until you arrive at a crossroads with a fuel station across the road. Turn right back onto New Mill Lane where you walk for 400m descending back to where you started.

Clumber Park,

The Estate Office, Worksop, Notts, S80 3AZ
Tel: 01909 476592 or 484977 (April – Oct)
Fax: 01909 500721
www.nationaltrust.org

Opening Times
Park - all year from dawn to dusk
Conservation Centre -
April – Sept, 1pm – 5pm on Sat, Sun
and Bank Holiday Mondays
Chapel - please phone for opening times
Cafeteria - daily
April – end of Oct, 10.30am – 6.00pm
Nov – end of March, 10.30am – 4.00pm
(closed 25 & 26 Dec)
Cycle Hire -
April – end of Oct, 10.00am – 4.00pm
Nov – end of March, 10.00am – 2.00pm

Creswell Crags Visitor Centre

Crags Road, Welbeck Worksop, Notts, S80 3LH
Tel: 01909 720378   Fax: 01909 813200

The Harley Gallery

A60 Mansfield Road, Welbeck, Worksop
Tel: 01909 501700
email: info@harleygallery.co.uk
www.harleygallery.co.uk

Newstead Abbey

Newstead Abbey, Ravenshead,
Nottinghamshire, NG15 8NA
Tel: 01623 455900   Fax: 01623 455904
www.newsteadabbey.org.uk

Rufford Abbey Country Park and Craft Centre

Ollerton, Nottinghamshire, NG22 9DF
Tel: 01623 822944
www.ruffordcraftcentre.org.uk

Sherwood Forest Country Park and Visitor Centre

Edwinstowe, Mansfield, Nottinghamshire, NG21 9HN
General Enquiries: events, group facilities
01623 823202
Visitor Information Centre (seasonal)
01623 824490
24 hour brochure line
01623 824317
www.sherwood-forest.org.uk

Opening times, Parking and Disabled Access
The Country Park is open daily, dawn to dusk.
The Visitor Centre is open daily,
April to Oct 10.30am – 5.00pm
Nov – March 10.30am – 4.30pm

Car parking charges apply at various times of the
year. Free coach parking and disabled badge holders.

Disabled Access: Surfaced paths to the Major Oak in
the heart of the forest. Good access to entire Visitor
Centre. Disabled toilet. Wheelchair and electric
vehicle available.

Sherwood Pines Forest Park

Forest Enterprise, Sherwood and Lincs. Forest District,
Edwinstowe, Nottinghamshire, NG21 9JL
Tel: 01623 822447
Sherwood Pines Visitor Centre. Tel: 01623 822500

Thoresby Hall Hotel,

Thoresby Park, Nr Perlethorpe,
Nottinghamshire, NG22 9WH
Tel: 01623 821000

The Thoresby Gallery

Thoresby Park, Ollerton, Newark,
Nottinghamshire, NG22 9EP
Tel: 01623 822365/822009

Worksop Priory Church and Gatehouse

The Priory Vicarage, Worksop, Notts, S80 2HY
Tel: 01909 472180

Opening Times - April – Sept,
Mon, Thurs, Sat - 9.00am – 12.00pm
Subject to guides availability (times may vary)
Gatehouse by appointment only.

Tourist Information Centres

Nottingham

1-4 Smithy Row, Nottingham, NG1 2BY
Tel: 0115 9155330
email: tourist.information@nottinghamcity.gov.uk

Ollerton

Sherwood Heath, Ollerton Roundabout, Ollerton,
Newark, Nottinghamshire, NG22 9DR
Tel: 01623 824545

Worksop

Worksop Library, Memorial Avenue, Worksop,
Nottinghamshire S80 2BP
Tel: 01909 501148
email: worksop.tourist@bassetlaw.gov.uk